11 STEPS ENGLISH WORKBOOK

The Easiest Way of Learning

CLASS-9

SUBHASH SHYAM SAHARSH

NOTION PRESS

NOTION PRESS

India. Singapore. Malaysia.

ISBN xxx-x-xxxxx-xx-x

TO MY BRIGHT AND CREATIVE LEARNERS

Contents

Preface

Since I started teaching in 2006 I felt the students understood the English text as per their previous knowledge. And here only the all game started. Those who came from well to do family were good enough to catch the eyes of the teacher in the class and those who came from a background of struggle, they did what they could and It was not enough if compared to the best performance in the class by those superior children.

This feeling somewhere created an inferior complex in their mind. That's why I got an idea which is far from any discrimination of fast or slow learners in the class. The every bit of this workbook makes the child familiar to the chapter in detail which they must understand.

The main aim of this workbook is to make the children-

- Self dependent
- Learn their own in their own comfort
- Master in self learning
- Clear of the topics in the prescribed syllabus

SUBHASH SHYAM SAHARSH

AUTHOR

SCHOOL

....

....

....

SESSION ....

NAME:...

CLASS/SEC ....

FAVOURITE SUBJECT ....

GOAL ....

MY IDEAL ....

MY STRENGTH ....

MY WEAKNESS ....

I DEFINE THE WORLD AS

....

....

....

....

....

....

AFFIRMATION

I AM GREATFUL FOR ALL I HAVE IN MY LIFE.

I AM WALKING TO MY GOAL OF MY LIFE.

I KNOW AND UNDERSTAND MY TOMORROW IS BRIGHT AND I WILL MAKE THE WORLD A BRIGHTER PLACE FOR THE COMFORT, PEACE AND POSITIVITY.

Acknowledgments

Whole heartedly I can say that this book is result of those all children with whom I shared the classroom learning and we understood the syllabus in the easier way by following 11 steps.

The 11 steps also kept changing from time to time as I observed I added something for their betterment only.

From time to time I received their feedback and came to know that they really enjoy it and they told the **11 steps Learning Method** is good. They could have done better if they had been taught in the same way since their junior classes

LET US UNDERSTAND 11 STEPS

1. READ THE CHAPTER (1ST TIME)
2. **WRITE** THE **NEW WORDS/HARD WORDS** FROM CHAPTER (WRITE THE MEANING OF THE WORD ALSO WITH THE HELP OF A DICTIONARY)
3. WRITE THE NAME OF-
    - **a) CHARACTER**
    - **b) PLACE**
    - **c) OBJECT**
4. WRITE **IMPROTANT INCIDENCES** (THE ORDERS WHAT HAPPENS IN THE CHAPTER)
5. **EXPLAIN** THE **PARAGRAPH** OF THE CHAPTER (MINIMUM IN 3-4 LINES EACH)
6. WRITE **SHORT SUMMARY** (IN **60-80 WORDS** BASED ON THE **IMPROTANT INCIDENCES**)
7. **MAKE SENTENCE** WITH THE NEW WORDS OF STEP NO. 2
8. **GIVE REASON** FOR YOU LIKED/DISLIKED THE CHAPTER
9. WRITE **QUESTION BANK (ONLY QUESTIONS)**
    - a) 5 SHORT QUESTIONS
    - b) 2 LONG QUESTONS
    - c) 10 MCQ
10. **READ THE CHAPTER 2ND TIME**
11. WRITE **LONG SUMMARY (80-100 WORDS)** BASED ON THE STEP NO. 4

***

11 STEPS SAMPLE

CHAPTER: THE ANT AND THE CRICKET (FOR UNDRESTANDING HOW TO DO)

1. READ THE CHAPTER (1ST TIME) –I HAVE READ THIS POEM
2. **WRITE** THE **NEW WORDS/HARD WORDS** FROM CHAPTER
   Accustomed- habitual
   Crumb- a small piece of bread
   Grant- give/allow
   Starvation- famishment
3. WRITE THE NAME OF-
    - **d) CHARACTER**
        - **The ant**
        - **The cricket**
    - **e) PLACE**
        - **Ground**
        - **Cricket's home**
        - **Shelter**
        - **Ant's home**

f) OBJECT
   - **Cupboard**
   - **Crumb**
   - **Flower**
   - **Leaf**
   - **Snow**
   - **Grain**
   - **Heart**

4. WRITE **IMPROTANT INCIDENCES** (THE ORDERS WHAT HAPPENS IN THE CHAPTER; points can be written as per paragraph/stanza each)
   - The jolly cricket sang whole day and night throughout the summer and spring
   - He found nothing to eat in his home when the jolly season was over
   - Having felt hunger he ran to the ant to have some food and to return tomorrow
   - The ant did not accept his request and turned him away
   - At last the poet says some crickets have two legs (humans) and some have four (insect)
5. **EXPLAIN** THE **PARAGRAPH** OF THE CHAPTER (MINIMUM IN 3-4 LINES EACH)
   - Stanza 1: There was a young silly cricket that enjoyed the summer and spring season and did not worry about his food gathering concern. And when winter came he found he had nothing to eat.
   - Stanza 2: When he saw there was nothing to eat in the house, no flower on the snow covered ground, not a leaf on a tree he worried what will happen to him with hunger.
   - Stanza 3: At last driven by hunger he decided to go to ant, which could help him. He was wet and trembling in the cold.
   - Stanza 4: He thought the ant would give him shelter and food to eat. He also wished to return all what he got tomorrow. If not he would die of starvation.
   - Stanza 5: He politely told to the ant that he needed food, he was his friend but the ant denied giving him food saying that they never lend.
   - Stanza 6: He tells the reason of storing no food. His heart was so happy that he sang in the beauty of nature. Then the ant says if he had sang the whole summer and spring, he should dance now in the winter.
   - Stanza 7: In the last stanza the poet tells us that this poem is not merely a fable but it is true story. Some people also behave like the cricket in the poem and go for lending and repent in their life later.
6. WRITE **SHORT SUMMARY** (IN **60-80 WORDS** BASED ON THE **IMPROTANT INCIDENCES**)

   There was a young Cricket who enjoyed during the summer and Spring Day in the beautiful nature but Never worried about the food gathering for his home while the ant went on gathering food for the winter. When the Seasons were over the cricket knew that he had no food and finally decided to go to the ant. But the ant did not help him. In the last stanza the poet tells us that the human beings also behave like the cricket.
7. **MAKE SENTENCE** WITH THE NEW WORDS OF STEP NO. 2 (underline the new word in a sentence)

   Accustomed- He was accustomed of sleeping in the open.

   Crumb- The beggar begged helplessly for a crumb before a broken house in the city.

   Grant- Shyama thought her boss would grant her 4 days leave.

Starvation- The ex-police officer died of <u>starvation</u>.

8. **GIVE REASON** FOR YOU LIKED/DISLIKED THE CHAPTER
   I liked this poem because it compels us to think of our life and simultaneously it encourages us to be a hard worker to lead our life in comfort.
9. WRITE **QUESTION BANK (ONLY QUESTIONS)**
   d) 5 SHORT QUESTIONS
      i. In which season did the cricket sing?
      ii. Why did he have anything to eat?
      iii. What was his condition when he left for the ant?
      iv. What had compelled him to ask food from the ant?
      v. Who are the two footed cricket?
   e) 2 LONG QUESTONS
      i. Did the cricket do right singing throughout the jolly seasons?
      ii. Was the ant good in driving the cricket away? Why?
   f) 10 MCQ
      i. What did the ant do in summer?
         a. Sang
         b. Dance
         c. Ran
         d. Swam
      ii. What was not there to eat?
         a. Chicken
         b. Pasta
         c. Milk
         d. Crumb
      iii. The ground was covered with-
         a. Gold
         b. Coal
         c. Dust
         d. Snow
      iv. When the cricket came to know about food he became-
         a. Glad
         b. Calm
         c. Angry
         d. Sad
      v. What made him bold?
         a. Fame
         b. Famine
         c. Fading thoughts
         d. Green crops
      vi. The ant was-
         a. Miser
         b. Kind
         c. Meek

d. Coward

vii. Who was to shelter the cricket?

a. His friend
b. No one
c. The kind ant
d. His parents

viii. What did he wish to?

a. Lend
b. Borrow
c. Burrow
d. Sing again

ix. Did the ant welcome cricket warmly?

a. Yes
b. No
c. Not sure
d. None of the above

x. Whom did the cricket try to convince?

a. The poet
b. The poetess
c. The ant
d. The forest king

10. **READ THE CHAPTER 2ND TIME:** I have read the chapter.
11. WRITE **LONG SUMMARY (80-100 WORDS)** BASED ON THE STEP NO. 4

There was a young Cricket who enjoyed during the summer and Spring Day in the beautiful nature but Never worried about the food gathering for his home while the ant went on gathering food for the winter. After sometime the Jolly Seasons were over and all of sudden the cricket came to know that he was without food and finally decided that he will go to the ant. When he reached the door of the ant's house he was denied for anything so the cricket had to return back without anything. In the last stanza the poet tells us that the human beings also behave like the cricket.

The Fun They Had

MORAL: The physical teachers can not be replaced by a mechanical teacher.

1. READ THE CHAPTER (1ST TIME)
2. **WRITE** THE **NEW WORDS/HARD WORDS** FROM CHAPTER

3. WRITE THE NAME OF-

CHARACTER

PLACE

OBJECT

4. WRITE **IMPROTANT INCIDENCES** (THE ORDERS WHAT HAPPENS IN THE CHAPTER)

5. **EXPLAIN** THE **PARAGRAPH** OF THE CHAPTER (MINIMUM IN 3-4 LINES EACH)

6. WRITE **SHORT SUMMARY** (IN **60-80 WORDS** BASED ON THE **IMPROTANT INCIDENCES**)

7. **MAKE SENTENCE** WITH THE NEW WORDS OF STEP NO. 2

8. **GIVE REASON** FOR YOU LIKED/DISLIKED THE CHAPTER

9. WRITE **QUESTION BANK (ONLY QUESTIONS)**

5 SHORT QUESTIONS

2 LONG QUESTONS

10 MCQ

10. **READ THE CHAPTER 2ND TIME**
11. WRITE **LONG SUMMARY (80-100 WORDS)** BASED ON THE STEP NO. 4

The Sound Of Music

I. EVELYN GLENNIE

MORAL: one can reach to his/her goal if they decide to defeat the obstacles of life.

1. READ THE CHAPTER (1ST TIME)
2. **WRITE** THE **NEW WORDS/HARD WORDS** FROM CHAPTER

3. WRITE THE NAME OF-

CHARACTER

PLACE

OBJECT

4. WRITE **IMPROTANT INCIDENCES** (THE ORDERS WHAT HAPPENS IN THE CHAPTER)

5. **EXPLAIN** THE **PARAGRAPH** OF THE CHAPTER (MINIMUM IN 3-4 LINES EACH)

6. WRITE **SHORT SUMMARY** (IN **60-80 WORDS** BASED ON THE **IMPROTANT INCIDENCES)**

7. **MAKE SENTENCE** WITH THE NEW WORDS OF STEP NO. 2

8. **GIVE REASON** FOR YOU LIKED/DISLIKED THE CHAPTER

9. WRITE **QUESTION BANK (ONLY QUESTIONS)**

5 SHORT QUESTIONS

2 LONG QUESTONS

10 MCQ

10. **READ THE CHAPTER 2ND TIME**
11. WRITE **LONG SUMMARY (80-100 WORDS)** BASED ON THE STEP NO. 4

II. BISMILLAH KHAN

MORAL: Love to nation is greater than all other comforts of life.

1. READ THE CHAPTER (1ST TIME)
2. **WRITE** THE **NEW WORDS/HARD WORDS** FROM CHAPTER

3. WRITE THE NAME OF-

CHARACTER

PLACE

OBJECT

4. WRITE **IMPROTANT INCIDENCES** (THE ORDERS WHAT HAPPENS IN THE CHAPTER)

5. **EXPLAIN** THE **PARAGRAPH** OF THE CHAPTER (MINIMUM IN 3-4 LINES EACH)

6. WRITE **SHORT SUMMARY** (IN **60-80 WORDS** BASED ON THE **IMPROTANT INCIDENCES**)

7. **MAKE SENTENCE** WITH THE NEW WORDS OF STEP NO. 2

8. **GIVE REASON** FOR YOU LIKED/DISLIKED THE CHAPTER

9. WRITE **QUESTION BANK (ONLY QUESTIONS)**

5 SHORT QUESTIONS

2 LONG QUESTONS

10 MCQ

10. **READ THE CHAPTER 2ND TIME**
11. WRITE **LONG SUMMARY (80-100 WORDS)** BASED ON THE STEP NO. 4

The Little Girl

MORAL: Our parents may be hard outside but they always love us.

1. READ THE CHAPTER (1ST TIME)
2. **WRITE** THE **NEW WORDS/HARD WORDS** FROM CHAPTER

3. WRITE THE NAME OF-

CHARACTER

PLACE

OBJECT

4. WRITE **IMPROTANT INCIDENCES** (THE ORDERS WHAT HAPPENS IN THE CHAPTER)

5. **EXPLAIN** THE **PARAGRAPH** OF THE CHAPTER (MINIMUM IN 3-4 LINES EACH)

6. WRITE **SHORT SUMMARY** (IN **60-80 WORDS** BASED ON THE **IMPROTANT INCIDENCES)**

7. **MAKE SENTENCE** WITH THE NEW WORDS OF STEP NO. 2

8. **GIVE REASON** FOR YOU LIKED/DISLIKED THE CHAPTER

9. WRITE **QUESTION BANK (ONLY QUESTIONS)**

5 SHORT QUESTIONS

2 LONG QUESTONS

10 MCQ

10. **READ THE CHAPTER 2ND TIME**
11. WRITE **LONG SUMMARY** (**80-100 WORDS**) BASED ON THE STEP NO. 4

A Truly Beautiful Mind

MORAL: A person can be great if he/she thinks of the humanity.

1. READ THE CHAPTER (1ST TIME)
2. **WRITE** THE **NEW WORDS/HARD WORDS** FROM CHAPTER

3. WRITE THE NAME OF-

CHARACTER

PLACE

OBJECT

4. WRITE **IMPROTANT INCIDENCES** (THE ORDERS WHAT HAPPENS IN THE CHAPTER)

5. **EXPLAIN** THE **PARAGRAPH** OF THE CHAPTER (MINIMUM IN 3-4 LINES EACH)

6. WRITE **SHORT SUMMARY** (IN **60-80 WORDS** BASED ON THE **IMPROTANT INCIDENCES**)

7. **MAKE SENTENCE** WITH THE NEW WORDS OF STEP NO. 2

8. **GIVE REASON** FOR YOU LIKED/DISLIKED THE CHAPTER

9. WRITE **QUESTION BANK (ONLY QUESTIONS)**

5 SHORT QUESTIONS

2 LONG QUESTONS

10 MCQ

10. **READ THE CHAPTER 2ND TIME**
11. WRITE **LONG SUMMARY (80-100 WORDS)** BASED ON THE STEP NO. 4

The Snake and the Mirror

MORAL: We should be very careful to deal with any situation in our life.

1. READ THE CHAPTER (1ST TIME)
2. **WRITE** THE **NEW WORDS/HARD WORDS** FROM CHAPTER

3. WRITE THE NAME OF-

CHARACTER

PLACE

OBJECT

4. WRITE **IMPROTANT INCIDENCES** (THE ORDERS WHAT HAPPENS IN THE CHAPTER)

5. **EXPLAIN** THE **PARAGRAPH** OF THE CHAPTER (MINIMUM IN 3-4 LINES EACH)

6. WRITE **SHORT SUMMARY** (IN **60-80 WORDS** BASED ON THE **IMPROTANT INCIDENCES**)

7. **MAKE SENTENCE** WITH THE NEW WORDS OF STEP NO. 2

8. **GIVE REASON** FOR YOU LIKED/DISLIKED THE CHAPTER

9. WRITE **QUESTION BANK (ONLY QUESTIONS)**

5 SHORT QUESTIONS

2 LONG QUESTONS

10 MCQ

10. **READ THE CHAPTER 2ND TIME**
11. WRITE **LONG SUMMARY (80-100 WORDS)** BASED ON THE STEP NO. 4

My Childhood

MORAL: Above all the religions comes the humanity first.

1. READ THE CHAPTER (1ST TIME)
2. **WRITE** THE **NEW WORDS/HARD WORDS** FROM CHAPTER

3. WRITE THE NAME OF-

CHARACTER

PLACE

OBJECT

4. WRITE **IMPROTANT INCIDENCES** (THE ORDERS WHAT HAPPENS IN THE CHAPTER)

5. **EXPLAIN** THE **PARAGRAPH** OF THE CHAPTER (MINIMUM IN 3-4 LINES EACH)

6. WRITE **SHORT SUMMARY** (IN **60-80 WORDS** BASED ON THE **IMPROTANT INCIDENCES)**

7. **MAKE SENTENCE** WITH THE NEW WORDS OF STEP NO. 2

8. **GIVE REASON** FOR YOU LIKED/DISLIKED THE CHAPTER

9. WRITE **QUESTION BANK (ONLY QUESTIONS)**

5 SHORT QUESTIONS

2 LONG QUESTONS

10 MCQ

10. **READ THE CHAPTER 2ND TIME**
11. WRITE **LONG SUMMARY (80-100 WORDS)** BASED ON THE STEP NO. 4

Reach For the Top

SANTOSH YADAV

MORAL: A person should listen to the call of heart always irrespective of all diversions.

1. READ THE CHAPTER (1ST TIME)
2. **WRITE** THE **NEW WORDS/HARD WORDS** FROM CHAPTER

3. WRITE THE NAME OF-

CHARACTER

PLACE

OBJECT

4. WRITE **IMPROTANT INCIDENCES** (THE ORDERS WHAT HAPPENS IN THE CHAPTER)

5. **EXPLAIN** THE **PARAGRAPH** OF THE CHAPTER (MINIMUM IN 3-4 LINES EACH)

6. WRITE **SHORT SUMMARY** (IN **60-80 WORDS** BASED ON THE **IMPROTANT INCIDENCES)**

7. **MAKE SENTENCE** WITH THE NEW WORDS OF STEP NO. 2

8. **GIVE REASON** FOR YOU LIKED/DISLIKED THE CHAPTER

9. WRITE **QUESTION BANK** (ONLY QUESTIONS)

5 SHORT QUESTIONS

2 LONG QUESTONS

10 MCQ

10. **READ THE CHAPTER 2ND TIME**
11. WRITE **LONG SUMMARY (80-100 WORDS)** BASED ON THE STEP NO. 4

Maria Sharapova

MORAL: One who lose something gets many things in return.

1. READ THE CHAPTER (1ST TIME)
2. **WRITE** THE **NEW WORDS/HARD WORDS** FROM CHAPTER

3. WRITE THE NAME OF-

CHARACTER

PLACE

OBJECT

4. WRITE **IMPROTANT INCIDENCES** (THE ORDERS WHAT HAPPENS IN THE CHAPTER)

5. **EXPLAIN** THE **PARAGRAPH** OF THE CHAPTER (MINIMUM IN 3-4 LINES EACH)

6. WRITE **SHORT SUMMARY** (IN **60-80 WORDS** BASED ON THE **IMPROTANT INCIDENCES)**

7. **MAKE SENTENCE** WITH THE NEW WORDS OF STEP NO. 2

8. **GIVE REASON** FOR YOU LIKED/DISLIKED THE CHAPTER

9. WRITE **QUESTION BANK (ONLY QUESTIONS)**

5 SHORT QUESTIONS

2 LONG QUESTONS

10 MCQ

10. **READ THE CHAPTER 2ND TIME**
11. WRITE **LONG SUMMARY (80-100 WORDS)** BASED ON THE STEP NO. 4

Kathmandu

MORAL: A person who visits different places gets more knowledge and understanding than those who not.

1. READ THE CHAPTER (1ST TIME)
2. **WRITE** THE **NEW WORDS/HARD WORDS** FROM CHAPTER

3. WRITE THE NAME OF-

CHARACTER

PLACE

OBJECT

4. WRITE **IMPROTANT INCIDENCES** (THE ORDERS WHAT HAPPENS IN THE CHAPTER)

5. **EXPLAIN** THE **PARAGRAPH** OF THE CHAPTER (MINIMUM IN 3-4 LINES EACH)

6. WRITE **SHORT SUMMARY** (IN **60-80 WORDS** BASED ON THE **IMPROTANT INCIDENCES**)

7. **MAKE SENTENCE** WITH THE NEW WORDS OF STEP NO. 2

8. **GIVE REASON** FOR YOU LIKED/DISLIKED THE CHAPTER

9. WRITE **QUESTION BANK (ONLY QUESTIONS)**

5 SHORT QUESTIONS

2 LONG QUESTONS

10 MCQ

10. **READ THE CHAPTER 2ND TIME**
11. WRITE **LONG SUMMARY (80-100 WORDS)** BASED ON THE STEP NO. 4

If I Were You

MORAL: We should not judge a person by his/her appearance, it may misguide us.

1. READ THE CHAPTER (1ST TIME)
2. **WRITE** THE **NEW WORDS/HARD WORDS** FROM CHAPTER

3. WRITE THE NAME OF-
CHARACTER

PLACE

OBJECT

4. WRITE **IMPROTANT INCIDENCES** (THE ORDERS WHAT HAPPENS IN THE CHAPTER)

5. **EXPLAIN** THE **PARAGRAPH** OF THE CHAPTER (MINIMUM IN 3-4 LINES EACH)

6. WRITE **SHORT SUMMARY** (IN **60-80 WORDS** BASED ON THE **IMPROTANT INCIDENCES)**

7. **MAKE SENTENCE** WITH THE NEW WORDS OF STEP NO. 2

8. **GIVE REASON** FOR YOU LIKED/DISLIKED THE CHAPTER

9. WRITE **QUESTION BANK (ONLY QUESTIONS)**

5 SHORT QUESTIONS

2 LONG QUESTONS

10 MCQ

10. **READ THE CHAPTER 2ND TIME**
11. WRITE **LONG SUMMARY (80-100 WORDS)** BASED ON THE STEP NO. 4

The Road Not Taken

MORAL: Be very careful while selecting the goal of your life.

1. READ THE CHAPTER (1ST TIME)
2. **WRITE** THE **NEW WORDS/HARD WORDS** FROM CHAPTER

3. WRITE THE NAME OF-

CHARACTER

PLACE

OBJECT

4. WRITE **IMPROTANT INCIDENCES** (THE ORDERS WHAT HAPPENS IN THE CHAPTER)

5. **EXPLAIN** THE **PARAGRAPH** OF THE CHAPTER (MINIMUM IN 3-4 LINES EACH)

6. WRITE **SHORT SUMMARY** (IN **60-80 WORDS** BASED ON THE **IMPROTANT INCIDENCES**)

7. **MAKE SENTENCE** WITH THE NEW WORDS OF STEP NO. 2

8. **GIVE REASON** FOR YOU LIKED/DISLIKED THE CHAPTER

9. WRITE **QUESTION BANK (ONLY QUESTIONS)**

5 SHORT QUESTIONS

2 LONG QUESTONS

10 MCQ

10. **READ THE CHAPTER 2ND TIME**
11. WRITE **LONG SUMMARY (80-100 WORDS)** BASED ON THE STEP NO. 4

Wind

MORAL: It is better to be strong to face the power of wind.

1. READ THE CHAPTER (1ST TIME)
2. **WRITE** THE **NEW WORDS/HARD WORDS** FROM CHAPTER

3. WRITE THE NAME OF-
CHARACTER

PLACE

OBJECT

4. WRITE **IMPROTANT INCIDENCES** (THE ORDERS WHAT HAPPENS IN THE CHAPTER)

5. **EXPLAIN** THE **PARAGRAPH** OF THE CHAPTER (MINIMUM IN 3-4 LINES EACH)

6. WRITE **SHORT SUMMARY** (IN **60-80 WORDS** BASED ON THE **IMPROTANT INCIDENCES)**

7. **MAKE SENTENCE** WITH THE NEW WORDS OF STEP NO. 2

8. **GIVE REASON** FOR YOU LIKED/DISLIKED THE CHAPTER

9. WRITE **QUESTION BANK (ONLY QUESTIONS)**

5 SHORT QUESTIONS

2 LONG QUESTONS

10 MCQ

10. **READ THE CHAPTER 2ND TIME**
11. WRITE **LONG SUMMARY (80-100 WORDS)** BASED ON THE STEP NO. 4

Rain On the Roof

MORAL: Our own is always our own they give us a sweet memory.

1. READ THE CHAPTER (1ST TIME)
2. **WRITE** THE **NEW WORDS/HARD WORDS** FROM CHAPTER

3. WRITE THE NAME OF-
CHARACTER

PLACE

OBJECT

4. WRITE **IMPROTANT INCIDENCES** (THE ORDERS WHAT HAPPENS IN THE CHAPTER)

5. **EXPLAIN** THE **PARAGRAPH** OF THE CHAPTER (MINIMUM IN 3-4 LINES EACH)

6. WRITE **SHORT SUMMARY** (IN **60-80 WORDS** BASED ON THE **IMPROTANT INCIDENCES)**

7. **MAKE SENTENCE** WITH THE NEW WORDS OF STEP NO. 2

8. **GIVE REASON** FOR YOU LIKED/DISLIKED THE CHAPTER

9. WRITE **QUESTION BANK (ONLY QUESTIONS)**

5 SHORT QUESTIONS

2 LONG QUESTONS

10 MCQ

10. **READ THE CHAPTER 2ND TIME**
11. WRITE **LONG SUMMARY (80-100 WORDS)** BASED ON THE STEP NO. 4

The Lake Isle of Innisfree

MORAL: The lap of nature is an abode to mental peace.

1. READ THE CHAPTER (1ST TIME)
2. **WRITE** THE **NEW WORDS/HARD WORDS** FROM CHAPTER

3. WRITE THE NAME OF-

CHARACTER

PLACE

OBJECT

4. WRITE **IMPROTANT INCIDENCES** (THE ORDERS WHAT HAPPENS IN THE CHAPTER)

5. **EXPLAIN** THE **PARAGRAPH** OF THE CHAPTER (MINIMUM IN 3-4 LINES EACH)

6. WRITE **SHORT SUMMARY** (IN **60-80 WORDS** BASED ON THE **IMPROTANT INCIDENCES)**

7. **MAKE SENTENCE** WITH THE NEW WORDS OF STEP NO. 2

8. **GIVE REASON** FOR YOU LIKED/DISLIKED THE CHAPTER

9. WRITE **QUESTION BANK (ONLY QUESTIONS)**

5 SHORT QUESTIONS

2 LONG QUESTONS

10 MCQ

10. **READ THE CHAPTER 2ND TIME**
11. WRITE **LONG SUMMARY (80-100 WORDS)** BASED ON THE STEP NO. 4

A Legend of the Northland

MORAL: We should be kind enough to help the needy one.

1. READ THE CHAPTER (1ST TIME)
2. **WRITE** THE **NEW WORDS/HARD WORDS** FROM CHAPTER

3. WRITE THE NAME OF-

CHARACTER

PLACE

OBJECT

4. WRITE **IMPROTANT INCIDENCES** (THE ORDERS WHAT HAPPENS IN THE CHAPTER)

5. **EXPLAIN** THE **PARAGRAPH** OF THE CHAPTER (MINIMUM IN 3-4 LINES EACH)

6. WRITE **SHORT SUMMARY** (IN **60-80 WORDS** BASED ON THE **IMPROTANT INCIDENCES**)

7. **MAKE SENTENCE** WITH THE NEW WORDS OF STEP NO. 2

8. **GIVE REASON** FOR YOU LIKED/DISLIKED THE CHAPTER

9. WRITE **QUESTION BANK (ONLY QUESTIONS)**

5 SHORT QUESTIONS

2 LONG QUESTONS

10 MCQ

10. **READ THE CHAPTER 2ND TIME**
11. WRITE **LONG SUMMARY (80-100 WORDS)** BASED ON THE STEP NO. 4

No Men Are Foreign

MORAL: The earth is one so all are same on the earth.

1. READ THE CHAPTER (1ST TIME)
2. **WRITE** THE **NEW WORDS/HARD WORDS** FROM CHAPTER

3. WRITE THE NAME OF-

CHARACTER

PLACE

OBJECT

4. WRITE **IMPROTANT INCIDENCES** (THE ORDERS WHAT HAPPENS IN THE CHAPTER)

5. **EXPLAIN** THE **PARAGRAPH** OF THE CHAPTER (MINIMUM IN 3-4 LINES EACH)

6. WRITE **SHORT SUMMARY** (IN **60-80 WORDS** BASED ON THE **IMPROTANT INCIDENCES)**

7. **MAKE SENTENCE** WITH THE NEW WORDS OF STEP NO. 2

8. **GIVE REASON** FOR YOU LIKED/DISLIKED THE CHAPTER

9. WRITE **QUESTION BANK (ONLY QUESTIONS)**

5 SHORT QUESTIONS

2 LONG QUESTONS

10 MCQ

10. **READ THE CHAPTER 2ND TIME**
11. WRITE **LONG SUMMARY (80-100 WORDS)** BASED ON THE STEP NO. 4

On Killing a Tree

MORAL: We should plant more trees to save the earth.

1. READ THE CHAPTER (1ST TIME)
2. **WRITE** THE **NEW WORDS/HARD WORDS** FROM CHAPTER

3. WRITE THE NAME OF-

CHARACTER

PLACE

OBJECT

4. WRITE **IMPROTANT INCIDENCES** (THE ORDERS WHAT HAPPENS IN THE CHAPTER)

5. **EXPLAIN** THE **PARAGRAPH** OF THE CHAPTER (MINIMUM IN 3-4 LINES EACH)

6. WRITE **SHORT SUMMARY** (IN **60-80 WORDS** BASED ON THE **IMPROTANT INCIDENCES)**

7. **MAKE SENTENCE** WITH THE NEW WORDS OF STEP NO. 2

8. **GIVE REASON** FOR YOU LIKED/DISLIKED THE CHAPTER

9. WRITE **QUESTION BANK (ONLY QUESTIONS)**

5 SHORT QUESTIONS

2 LONG QUESTONS

10 MCQ

10. **READ THE CHAPTER 2ND TIME**
11. WRITE **LONG SUMMARY (80-100 WORDS)** BASED ON THE STEP NO. 4

A Slumber Did My Spirit Seal

MORAL: The loss of our own gives us a lot of pain.

1. READ THE CHAPTER (1ST TIME)
2. **WRITE** THE **NEW WORDS/HARD WORDS** FROM CHAPTER

3. WRITE THE NAME OF-

CHARACTER

PLACE

OBJECT

4. WRITE **IMPROTANT INCIDENCES** (THE ORDERS WHAT HAPPENS IN THE CHAPTER)

5. **EXPLAIN** THE **PARAGRAPH** OF THE CHAPTER (MINIMUM IN 3-4 LINES EACH)

6. WRITE **SHORT SUMMARY** (IN **60-80 WORDS** BASED ON THE **IMPROTANT INCIDENCES**)

7. **MAKE SENTENCE** WITH THE NEW WORDS OF STEP NO. 2

8. **GIVE REASON** FOR YOU LIKED/DISLIKED THE CHAPTER

9. WRITE **QUESTION BANK (ONLY QUESTIONS)**

5 SHORT QUESTIONS

2 LONG QUESTONS

10 MCQ

10. **READ THE CHAPTER 2ND TIME**
11. WRITE **LONG SUMMARY (80-100 WORDS)** BASED ON THE STEP NO. 4

The Lost Child

MORAL: Parents must be careful for the child in a crowded place.

1. READ THE CHAPTER (1ST TIME)
2. **WRITE** THE **NEW WORDS/HARD WORDS** FROM CHAPTER

3. WRITE THE NAME OF-

CHARACTER

PLACE

OBJECT

4. WRITE **IMPROTANT INCIDENCES** (THE ORDERS WHAT HAPPENS IN THE CHAPTER)

5. **EXPLAIN** THE **PARAGRAPH** OF THE CHAPTER (MINIMUM IN 3-4 LINES EACH)

6. WRITE **SHORT SUMMARY** (IN **60-80 WORDS** BASED ON THE **IMPROTANT INCIDENCES)**

7. **MAKE SENTENCE** WITH THE NEW WORDS OF STEP NO. 2

8. **GIVE REASON** FOR YOU LIKED/DISLIKED THE CHAPTER

9. WRITE **QUESTION BANK (ONLY QUESTIONS)**

5 SHORT QUESTIONS

2 LONG QUESTONS

10 MCQ

10. **READ THE CHAPTER 2ND TIME**
11. WRITE **LONG SUMMARY (80-100 WORDS)** BASED ON THE STEP NO. 4

The Adventures of Toto

MORAL: Wild animals must be left in their natural abode to live life freely.

1. READ THE CHAPTER (1ST TIME)
2. **WRITE** THE **NEW WORDS/HARD WORDS** FROM CHAPTER

3. WRITE THE NAME OF-

CHARACTER

PLACE

OBJECT

4. WRITE **IMPROTANT INCIDENCES** (THE ORDERS WHAT HAPPENS IN THE CHAPTER)

5. **EXPLAIN** THE **PARAGRAPH** OF THE CHAPTER (MINIMUM IN 3-4 LINES EACH)

6. WRITE **SHORT SUMMARY** (IN **60-80 WORDS** BASED ON THE **IMPROTANT INCIDENCES)**

7. **MAKE SENTENCE** WITH THE NEW WORDS OF STEP NO. 2

8. **GIVE REASON** FOR YOU LIKED/DISLIKED THE CHAPTER

9. WRITE **QUESTION BANK (ONLY QUESTIONS)**

5 SHORT QUESTIONS

2 LONG QUESTONS

10 MCQ

10. **READ THE CHAPTER 2ND TIME**
11. WRITE **LONG SUMMARY (80-100 WORDS)** BASED ON THE STEP NO. 4

Iswaran the Storyteller

MORAL: We should not be superstitious.

1. READ THE CHAPTER (1ST TIME)

2. **WRITE** THE **NEW WORDS/HARD WORDS** FROM CHAPTER

3. WRITE THE NAME OF-

CHARACTER

PLACE

OBJECT

4. WRITE **IMPROTANT INCIDENCES** (THE ORDERS WHAT HAPPENS IN THE CHAPTER)

5. **EXPLAIN** THE **PARAGRAPH** OF THE CHAPTER (MINIMUM IN 3-4 LINES EACH)

6. WRITE **SHORT SUMMARY** (IN **60-80 WORDS** BASED ON THE **IMPROTANT INCIDENCES**)

7. **MAKE SENTENCE** WITH THE NEW WORDS OF STEP NO. 2

8. **GIVE REASON** FOR YOU LIKED/DISLIKED THE CHAPTER

9. WRITE **QUESTION BANK (ONLY QUESTIONS)**

5 SHORT QUESTIONS

2 LONG QUESTONS

10 MCQ

10. **READ THE CHAPTER 2ND TIME**
11. WRITE **LONG SUMMARY (80-100 WORDS)** BASED ON THE STEP NO. 4

In The Kingdom Of Fools

MORAL: A foolish person more dangerous than any danger.

1. READ THE CHAPTER (1ST TIME)
2. **WRITE** THE **NEW WORDS/HARD WORDS** FROM CHAPTER

3. WRITE THE NAME OF-

CHARACTER

PLACE

OBJECT

4. WRITE **IMPROTANT INCIDENCES** (THE ORDERS WHAT HAPPENS IN THE CHAPTER)

5. **EXPLAIN** THE **PARAGRAPH** OF THE CHAPTER (MINIMUM IN 3-4 LINES EACH)

6. WRITE **SHORT SUMMARY** (IN **60-80 WORDS** BASED ON THE **IMPROTANT INCIDENCES)**

7. **MAKE SENTENCE** WITH THE NEW WORDS OF STEP NO. 2

8. **GIVE REASON** FOR YOU LIKED/DISLIKED THE CHAPTER

9. WRITE **QUESTION BANK (ONLY QUESTIONS)**

5 SHORT QUESTIONS

2 LONG QUESTONS

10 MCQ

10. **READ THE CHAPTER 2ND TIME**
11. WRITE **LONG SUMMARY (80-100 WORDS)** BASED ON THE STEP NO. 4

The Happy Prince

MORAL: Kindness is always a blessing to humanity.

1. READ THE CHAPTER (1ST TIME)
2. **WRITE** THE **NEW WORDS/HARD WORDS** FROM CHAPTER

3. WRITE THE NAME OF-

CHARACTER

PLACE

OBJECT

4. WRITE **IMPROTANT INCIDENCES** (THE ORDERS WHAT HAPPENS IN THE CHAPTER)

5. **EXPLAIN** THE **PARAGRAPH** OF THE CHAPTER (MINIMUM IN 3-4 LINES EACH)

6. WRITE **SHORT SUMMARY** (IN **60-80 WORDS** BASED ON THE **IMPROTANT INCIDENCES)**

7. **MAKE SENTENCE** WITH THE NEW WORDS OF STEP NO. 2

8. **GIVE REASON** FOR YOU LIKED/DISLIKED THE CHAPTER

9. WRITE **QUESTION BANK (ONLY QUESTIONS)**

5 SHORT QUESTIONS

2 LONG QUESTONS

10 MCQ

10. **READ THE CHAPTER 2ND TIME**
11. WRITE **LONG SUMMARY (80-100 WORDS)** BASED ON THE STEP NO. 4

The Last Leaf

MORAL: An optimistic view of life can give more peace and happiness than a pessimistic view.

1. READ THE CHAPTER (1ST TIME)
2. **WRITE** THE **NEW WORDS/HARD WORDS** FROM CHAPTER

3. WRITE THE NAME OF-

CHARACTER

PLACE

OBJECT

4. WRITE **IMPROTANT INCIDENCES** (THE ORDERS WHAT HAPPENS IN THE CHAPTER)

5. **EXPLAIN** THE **PARAGRAPH** OF THE CHAPTER (MINIMUM IN 3-4 LINES EACH)

6. WRITE **SHORT SUMMARY** (IN **60-80 WORDS** BASED ON THE **IMPROTANT INCIDENCES)**

7. **MAKE SENTENCE** WITH THE NEW WORDS OF STEP NO. 2

8. **GIVE REASON** FOR YOU LIKED/DISLIKED THE CHAPTER

9. WRITE **QUESTION BANK (ONLY QUESTIONS)**

5 SHORT QUESTIONS

2 LONG QUESTONS

10 MCQ

10. **READ THE CHAPTER 2ND TIME**
11. WRITE **LONG SUMMARY (80-100 WORDS)** BASED ON THE STEP NO. 4

A House Is Not a Home

MORAL: Our house is the most peaceful and safest place in the world.

1. READ THE CHAPTER (1ST TIME)
2. **WRITE** THE **NEW WORDS/HARD WORDS** FROM CHAPTER

3. WRITE THE NAME OF-

CHARACTER

PLACE

OBJECT

4. WRITE **IMPROTANT INCIDENCES** (THE ORDERS WHAT HAPPENS IN THE CHAPTER)

5. **EXPLAIN** THE **PARAGRAPH** OF THE CHAPTER (MINIMUM IN 3-4 LINES EACH)

6. WRITE **SHORT SUMMARY** (IN **60-80 WORDS** BASED ON THE **IMPROTANT INCIDENCES)**

7. **MAKE SENTENCE** WITH THE NEW WORDS OF STEP NO. 2

8. **GIVE REASON** FOR YOU LIKED/DISLIKED THE CHAPTER

9. WRITE **QUESTION BANK (ONLY QUESTIONS)**

5 SHORT QUESTIONS

2 LONG QUESTONS

10 MCQ

10. **READ THE CHAPTER 2ND TIME**
11. WRITE **LONG SUMMARY (80-100 WORDS)** BASED ON THE STEP NO. 4

The Beggar

MORAL: Love and care has power to change a bad man also.

1. READ THE CHAPTER (1ST TIME)
2. **WRITE** THE **NEW WORDS/HARD WORDS** FROM CHAPTER

3. WRITE THE NAME OF-
CHARACTER

PLACE

OBJECT

4. WRITE **IMPROTANT INCIDENCES** (THE ORDERS WHAT HAPPENS IN THE CHAPTER)

5. **EXPLAIN** THE **PARAGRAPH** OF THE CHAPTER (MINIMUM IN 3-4 LINES EACH)

6. WRITE **SHORT SUMMARY** (IN **60-80 WORDS** BASED ON THE **IMPROTANT INCIDENCES)**

7. **MAKE SENTENCE** WITH THE NEW WORDS OF STEP NO. 2

8. **GIVE REASON** FOR YOU LIKED/DISLIKED THE CHAPTER

9. WRITE **QUESTION BANK (ONLY QUESTIONS)**

5 SHORT QUESTIONS

2 LONG QUESTONS

10 MCQ

10. **READ THE CHAPTER 2ND TIME**
11. WRITE **LONG SUMMARY (80-100 WORDS)** BASED ON THE STEP NO. 4

Printed by Libri Plureos GmbH in Hamburg,
Germany